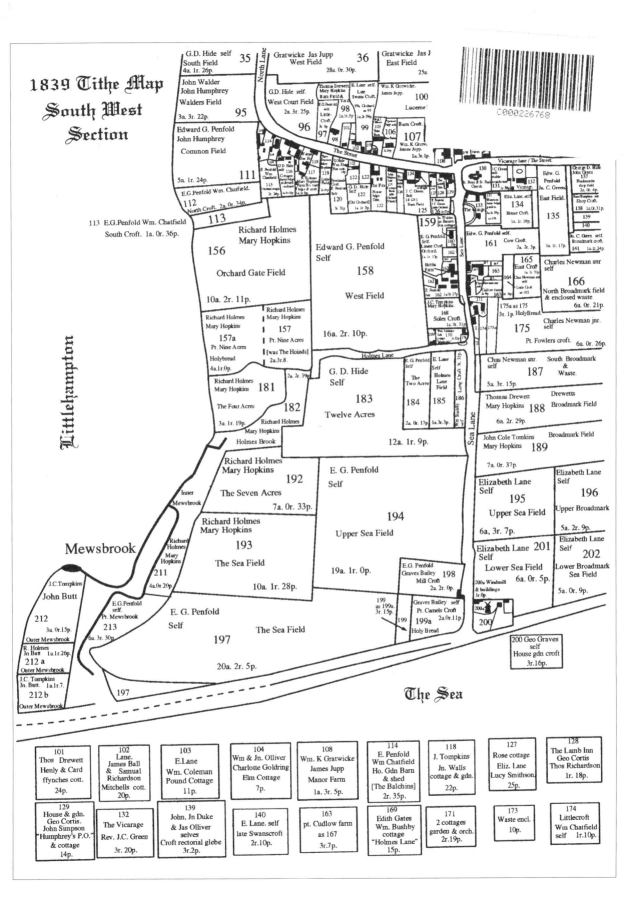

# 1839 Tithe Map South West Section

**The Sea**

**Mewsbrook**

Littlehampton

*Map parcels and owners:*

G.D. Hide self / South Field / 4a. 1r. 26p. — **35**

Gratwicke Jas Jupp / West Field — **36**

Gratwicke Jas J... / East Field / 25a. — (100 area)

John Walder / John Humphrey / Walders Field / 3a. 3r. 22p. — **95**

G.D. Hide self. / West Court Field / 2a. 3r. 25p. — **96**

Thomas Drewett / Mary Hopkins / Barn Field & / Yard — **98**

E. Lane self. / Lane / Swanscroft. — (99)

Wm. K Gratwicke / James Jupp. — **100**

Luceme... — (100)

Edward G. Penfold / John Humphrey / Common Field / 5a. 1r. 24p. — **111**

**97 98 99 106 107** Barn Croft / Wm. K Gratwicke / James Jupp. / 1a. 3r. 1p.

E.G.Penfold Wm. Chatfield — **112**

113 E.G.Penfold Wm Chatfield / South Croft. 1a. 0r. 36p.

North Croft. 2a. 0r. 34p. — **113**

Richard Holmes / Mary Hopkins / Orchard Gate Field / 10a. 2r. 11p. — **156**

Edward G. Penfold / Self / West Field / 16a. 2r. 10p. — **158**

Richard Holmes / Mary Hopkins / Pt. Nine Acres / Holybread / 4a. 1r. 0p. — **157a**

Richard Holmes / Mary Hopkins / Pt. Nine Acres / [was The Hoinds] / 2a. 3r. 8. — **157**

E. G. Penfold / Self / Orchard. — **159**

Soles Croft. / 1a. 0r. 36p. — **168**

Edw. G. Penfold self — **161**

Cow Croft. / 2a. 0r. 3p. — (161)

Charles Newman snr / self — **165** East Croft

Charles Newman snr / self / North Broadmark field / & enclosed waste / 6a. 0r. 21p. — **166**

Charles Newman jnr. / self / Pt. Fowlers croft. / 6a. 0r. 26p. — **175**

Edw. G. / Penfold / Jn. C. Green — (137) East Field.

George D. Hide / John Green / Blacksmiths shop field / 2a. 0r. 4p. — **137**

Wm. Humphrey self / Shop Croft / 1a. 0r. 31p. — **138**

— **139 140 141** Jn. C. Green self. / Broadmark croft / 1a. 1r. 24p.

Elizabeth Lane self / House Croft. / 1a. 1r. 18p. — **134**

— **135**

Richard Holmes / Mary Hopkins / Pt. Nine Acres / 157a

Richard Holmes / Mary Hopkins / The Four Acres / 3a. 1r. 19p. — **181**

Richard Holmes / Mary Hopkins / 182

G. D. Hide / Self / Twelve Acres / 12a. 1r. 9p. — **183**

G. D. Hide / Self / The Two Acres / 2a. 0r. 17p. — **184**

E. Lane / Self / Holmes / Lane / Field / 1a. 3r. 3p. — **185**

Holmes Lane

Holmes Brook

E. G. Penfold / Self — (184 area)

— **186**

Chas Newman snr / self / 5a. 3r. 15p. — **187** South Broadmark & Waste.

Thomas Drewett / Mary Hopkins / 6a. 2r. 29p. — **188** Drewetts / Broadmark Field

Richard Holmes / Mary Hopkins / The Seven Acres / 7a. 0r. 33p. — **192**

E. G. Penfold / Self — **194** Upper Sea Field / 19a. 1r. 0p.

Richard Holmes / Mary Hopkins / The Sea Field / 10a. 1r. 28p. — **193**

John Cole Tomkins / Mary Hopkins / 7a. 0r. 37p. — **189** Broadmark Field

Elizabeth Lane / Self / Upper Sea Field / 6a. 3r. 7p. — **195**

Elizabeth Lane / Self / Upper Broadmark / 5a. 2r. 9p. — **196**

Elizabeth Lane / Self / Lower Sea Field / 6a. 0r. 5p. — **201**

Elizabeth Lane / Self / Lower Broadmark / Sea Field / 5a. 0r. 9p. — **202**

Inner Mewsbrook

Richard Holmes / Mary Hopkins / 4a.0r.20p. — **211**

E.G.Penfold self. / Pt. Mewsbrook / 6a. 3r. 30p. — **213**

J.C.Tompkins / John Butt / 3a. 0r.15p. — **212** Outer Mewsbrook

R. Holmes / Jn Butt / 1a.1r.26p. — **212 a** Outer Mewsbrook

J.C. Tompkins / Jn. Butt. / 1a.1r.7. — **212 b** Outer Mewsbrook

E. G. Penfold / Self — **197** The Sea Field / 20a. 2r. 5p.

197

E.G. Penfold / Graves Bailey / Mill Croft / 2a. 0r. 0p. — **198**

199 us 199u / 3r. 15p. — (199)

Graves Bailey self / Pt. Camels Croft / 2a.0r.11p. / Holy Bread — **199a** — **199**

200a Windmill / & buildings / 1r.0p. — **200a**

200 Geo Graves / self / House gdn croft / 3r.16p. — **200**

---

**101** / Thos Drewett / Henly & Card / ffynches cott. / 24p.

**102** / Lane. / James Ball & / Samual / Richardson / Mitchells cott. / 20p.

**103** / E.Lane / Wm. Coleman / Pound Cottage / 11p.

**104** / Wm & Jn. Olliver / Charlotte Goldring / Elm Cottage / 7p.

**108** / Wm. K Gratwicke / James Jupp / Manor Farm / 1a. 3r. 5p.

**114** / E. Penfold / Wm Chatfield / Ho. Gdn Barn / & shed / [The Balchins] / 2r. 35p.

**118** / J. Tompkins / Jn. Walls / cottage & gdn. / 22p.

**127** / Rose cottage / Eliz. Lane / Lucy Smithson / 25p.

**128** / The Lamb Inn / Geo Cortis / Thos Richardson / 1r. 18p.

**129** / House & gdn. / Geo Cortis. / John Simpson / "Humphrey's P.O." / & cottage / 14p.

**132** / The Vicarage / Rev. J.C. Green / 3r. 20p.

**139** / John, Jn Duke / & Jas Olliver / selves / Croft rectorial glebe / 3r.2p.

**140** / E. Lane. self / late Swanscroft / 2r.10p.

**163** / pt. Cudlow farm / as 167 / 3r.7p.

**169** / Edith Gates / Wm. Bushby / cottage / "Holmes Lane" / 15p.

**171** / 2 cottages / garden & orch. / 2r.19p.

**173** / Waste encl. / 10p.

**174** / Littlecroft / Wm Chatfield / self / 1r.10p.

# RUSTINGTON
## A Pictorial History

Rustington Mill

# RUSTINGTON
## A Pictorial History

Mary Taylor

*Best Wishes*
*Mary Taylor*

**Phillimore**

1998

Published by
PHILLIMORE & CO. LTD.
Shopwyke Manor Barn, Chichester, West Sussex

ISBN 1 86077 073 8

Printed and bound in Great Britain by
BIDDLES LTD.
Guildford, Surrey

*I would like to dedicate this book to my husband Bev,*
*our two sons, Andrew and Graeme and their families, with my love.*

# List of Illustrations

*Frontispiece:* Rustington Mill

# *Acknowledgements*

I would like to thank Beckett Newspapers, for permission to use the Neville Duke photograph no. 60, and also Middleton Press, for permission to use 'The Hoover Express' photograph, no. 25. Photographs nos. 81 and 82 are by kind permission of the United States Archives, Washington. I am also grateful to Mr. and Mrs. J.H. Manning, late of Smuggler's Nursery, for their interest, as well as the valuable information about nurseries in the village and the glass-house crops. I wish also to thank Tony Chapman for passing on information about Rustington which he has found while researching local newspapers.

My thanks are also due to Graeme, my son, for all the help he has given me. However, most of the credit for this book must be given to my husband, Bev. Apart from his help with the research, he has spent long hours coming to terms with his computer, as well as endeavouring to transcribe my hand-written scripts in time for publication. His patience and encouragement have always been there when I have needed them — Thank you, Bev.

# *Introduction*

**Early History**

Rustington, a village set between the South Downs and the sea, seems to have been inhabited from very early times, judging by the many archaeological artifacts that are constantly being found within its boundaries. The fertile soil of this coastal plain, with the forests to the north and the sea to the south, made Rustington a very attractive and safe place to live. There was also plenty of water from the springs, the tidal Black Ditch and an ample supply of salt.

In 1986, the author and her husband were called in to inspect one small area of a perimeter trench (dug to prevent access by travellers) around a field, now the site of Sainsbury's. Their findings prompted them to call in David Rudling and his colleagues from The Institute of Archaeology, University College, London, who undertook a rescue dig on the site. This was to lead to further rescue digs, along the then proposed Rustington bypass.

These sites revealed previously unrecorded archaeological features, artefactual evidence from the Mesolithic, Bronze and Iron ages, and also from the Early Roman and later medieval periods. The finds included flint tools, implements, pots, cooking vessels, glass, coins and a copper alloy brooch. Post holes where their houses (some with chalk floors) had stood were also found. Most exciting were the traces of a Roman tidal mill and a causeway together with evidence of a fishery. Tree trunks that were dug up at the time were dated (by dendrochronology at The University of Sheffield) between 2835-2620 B.C.

Following the Roman withdrawal from these shores in A.D. 436, there came the Saxon invaders from Germany. They set up their settlements all along the coastal plains and river valleys. We have significant evidence of settlements established here in the village. It is possible that Rustington acquired its name about this time; it is certainly of Saxon origin. The Danes attempted frequent raids along this part of the coast. However the Saxon settlements here were hardly ever disturbed, and life stayed unchanged for centuries.

All was to change after the Norman Conquest in 1066. The village then became one of the estates given to Roger de Montgomerie by William the Conqueror. This brought the feudal system to Rustington, with a succession of Lords of the Manor.

Savaric Fitzcane was given the Manor by King Henry I in 1102. Savaric's grandson was confirmed in his tenure of the Manor by Richard I in 1190. Then in the 13th century there came the infamous de Bohuns, who were well known for abusing their rights, privileges and powers. After them the change of ownership becomes complicated, with descent through the female line. The Manor was divided into Rustington West Court and Rustington East Court.

Here is an extract from the archives of Althorp in Northamptonshire, later the home of Diana, Princess of Wales, appertaining to Rustington:

Some other well-known names associated with the lordship of the manors, were — Bramshott, Barford, Viscount de Lisle, Cooke, Bannister, Palmer, Sir Hugh Acland and the Dukes of Richmond and Norfolk. The last Lord of the Manor was William Kinleside Gratwick of Ham, Angmering — he died in 1862 and, with his death, the way of life in the village again changed.

### 19th- and 20th-Century Rustington

Rustington was always essentially a farming community, with several dairy farms and crop-producing farms. Midway through the 19th century, a combination of events changed the way of life of the folk of Rustington. The death of the last Lord of the Manor and the mechanisation of farming, which led to a loss of jobs for farm labourers, meant that new work had to be found.

At this time brickfields were being opened in Rustington, which required workers, and helped the employment situation. The first known brickfield was in 1867, east of Ash Lane, followed by several on both sides of Worthing Road. The last to open and,

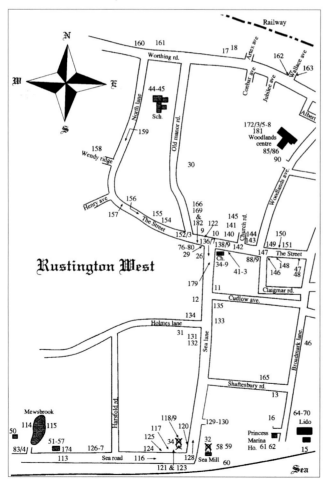

Figures on the maps correspond to illustrations throughout the book.

incidentally, the last to close, in 1948, was in North Lane. Mr. James Linfield of Littlehampton, one of the brickfield owners, had houses built for his workers in Worthing and Albert roads (*c*.1897-1907). The houses are still occupied.

The coming of the railway in 1846 was another factor in the change. This made the journey between London and the coast, much quicker and more convenient, so more people wanted to live here. The effect was that new houses had to be built, more bricks were needed, more labour required.

Rustington's first shop was opened by Mr. Simpson in 1846. He sold everything you could want, apart from drapery. The business was taken over by the Humphrey family. Mrs. Mary Ann Humphrey opened the first sub-post office in this shop in 1870, and in 1913 it became Rustington's first telephone call office. The shop stands in Sea Lane opposite the church, and the building is still there today.

Property developers also saw an opportunity in Rustington. Farm land was sold for building, and new roads and houses sprang up to cater for demand. Mr. Charles J. Drake built in Church Road and The Street, and Mr. Thomas Summers in Waverley, Glenville, Claigmar and Shaftesbury roads. They were among the first entrepreneurs to realise the potential of property.

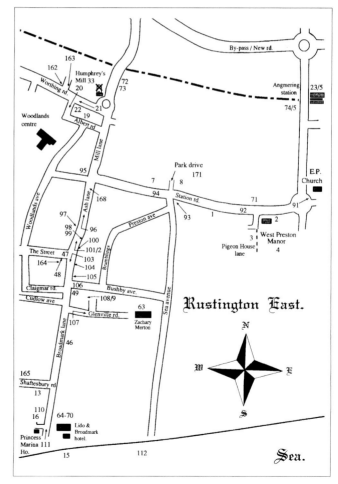

Mr. Summers was also responsible, during 1909, for building Broadway Mansions on the corner of The Street and Claigmar Road. These were the first purpose-built shops, over which nine apartments, on two storeys, were built. (These are now demolished and Sterling Parade is on the site.)

Some of the farmland was taken over by nurserymen. Over a dozen nurseries opened, producing glasshouse crops, which also eased the labour situation. All varieties of salad produce were grown; in particular, tomatoes and mushrooms, and exotic fruits and flowers.

## Windmills

At one period Rustington had three working windmills. The earliest of them was situated to the north of the village, at the junction of Worthing Road, Mill Lane, and New Road. This mill, a post mill, had been known during its lifetime as Drewett's Mill, Humphrey's Mill and Bridge Mill, c.1615-1896.

A second mill, a turret post mill, stood at the south-east corner of Sea Lane (now Overstrand Estate). It was called Sea Mill, 1821-1913.

The third mill, which only stood for a short time (1848-57), was in the field on the west side of Sea Lane. This mill was an open trestle post mill, and was removed bodily to Fishbourne in October 1857.

## Rustington Parish Church

It is possible that there was a church in Rustington before 1066. The very shape of the churchyard suggests that originally it was circular, typical of the Saxon period. The church would have been made of wattle and daub and thatched.

The first stone church would have been built sometime after 1066, under the jurisdiction of Earl Roger de Montgomerie. Earl Roger had a castle built for himself at nearby Arundel, when he became the first Earl of Arundel 1070-94. He imported the stone for his castle and churches from Caen in Normandy. Very little of this stone church now remains, having been altered and enlarged in the 12th and 13th centuries. The church, dedicated to St Peter and St Paul, is in a mixture of architectural styles, but is mostly Early English.

The tower dates from 1170 and is typical of its period. The date '1661', picked out in red brick near the top of the tower, indicates when the battlements were added.

The south arcade also dates from 1170 and is an excellent example of Transitional Norman architecture. The capitals on the pillars are very odd, and interesting.

The chancel is in the Early English style of about 1210. On the eastern face of the chancel arch are two shallow recesses that are worthy of note. There is a squint, which communicates with the Manorial/Lady Chapel. The chancel has an unusual, shuttered 'low-side' window. Apart from two circles of very old glass in a chancel window, all the stained glass is Victorian.

Two curious stone heads adorn the eastern arch into the Lady Chapel, from where you may also notice an opening near the chancel arch, with steps that once gave access to the rood loft.

The font is not the original one; this one dates from the 13th century. The font cover is Victorian and made of wood. Above hangs a gilded dove that is rather an unusual feature.

In 1992, the Lady Chapel floor was found to be suffering from wet rot and, while the floor was up for renovation, local archaeologists were invited to investigate. Six grave slabs were found, obviously not in their original resting places, and discovered beneath two of them was the original stone mensa [altar]. It had been smashed in half at the time of the Reformation, and the consecrational crosses, one at each corner, had been broken, though the central one was still clearly visible. The broken pieces were removed with difficulty, due to their weight and condition, and the altar top was then cleaned, measured, drawn and photographed. At a PCC meeting on 26 January 1993 it was resolved that the pieces of mensa/altar top should be placed under the new chapel floor, with an inspection cover over it. The historical connections with the Lady Chapel were thereby retained, and at the same time the stone was preserved.

The church has north and west porches of medieval origin and both have been skilfully restored.

More recently, during the 1939-45 war, the church was required to take part in the black-out. This was to stop light appearing outside, which might help enemy aircraft to navigate. Among the records of church expenditure for 1939-40 appears the following entry: 'To blacking out the church, and the necessary materials £2 5s. 1d. [225p]'

From the parish magazine during 1940, there was an important announcement to local blood donors:

> In the event of a serious local air-raid, all blood donors in class O are requested to watch the church tower for a red flag with a letter B. When this flag is raised, they shall report at Moot House, at ABC Corner, Rustington, at 10am the following morning without fail. Please note — the flag will be hoisted under police and military regulations.

Outside, on the north wall of the tower, is a single-handed clock dating from 1769. The clock was made in Marlborough, Wiltshire, and was used in Great Bedwyn church for about 100 years. In need of major repair, it was dismantled and removed, to be sold for what it could fetch — £2 0s. 0d. The purchaser was the Rev. E.J. Norris, vicar of a church in Reading, who happened to be a friend of one of the churchwardens of Rustington church. They needed a clock, so this ancient one was restored and fitted to the tower in 1905. The original circular iron face was removed and replaced by a square one, designed by Sir Ninian Comper. The present face is its fifth and is made of oak. The clock dial measures three feet in diameter. The solid brass hand is two feet long and weighs approximately 2lb. 6oz.

The picturesque lychgate was constructed from some old roof timbers, removed from the church at the time of its restoration in 1860. This replaced the five-bar farm gate which had stood there previously.

The church registers commenced in 1568. They show only too clearly when the Black Death swept through the village. The epidemic of 1597-99 caused 32 deaths to be recorded. In 1609, 21 villagers died, 15 of them within three months, while in 1670-71 the toll was 36 folk, as compared with an annual average death rate of four.

## Rustington's Sunday School

In 1825, the Rev. J.C. Green started the first Sunday School in the village. It was held, not in the church as you would expect, but in the largest room at the *Lamb Inn*. The superintendent of the school was the pub landlord, Mr. Thomas Richardson. In 1844 the Sunday school was transferred to another unlikely home, the annexe of the village smithy, which stood on the corner of The Street and Broadmark Lane. The superintendent then was the village blacksmith, Mr. John Green. Here it remained until the Church School was built next to the church in 1859.

## A Century for the National School

In 1859, the Rev. Henry J. Rush bought a piece of freehold land from the executors of the previous vicar, the Rev. J.C. Green, for £50. This land was situated between the old vicarage (now Abbots Lodge and Friars) and the churchyard. He employed a London architect, William Slater, to design a school and a school house and these plans are now deposited in the West Sussex Record Office at Chichester.

The Rev. Rush paid for the building himself, apart from a grant of £10 that he received from the Board of Education. When the building was completed on 5 June 1859, he conveyed, as a gift to the vicar, churchwardens and to the parish of Rustington, the school, the school house, and the land on which it stood.

Two date stones are set in the walls of the school house. One reads 'National School A.D. 1859', while the other reads 'E.M.R. A.D.1859'. These are the initials of the wife of the Rev. Rush, Elizabeth Martindale Rush, who died on 31 August 1859, aged 37.

The population in Rustington was about 345 at this time, and the school was built to accommodate 63 children. The average attendance was in fact 46 children, whose ages ranged from five to eleven years old.

By the turn of the century the population had almost doubled, so the school had to be enlarged. The cost of rebuilding had to be raised by the school itself. For several years they put on fund-raising concerts and plays, and the school building was enlarged in 1912, to accommodate 160 pupils.

During the six months of rebuilding, the children had their lessons at *The Lamb Inn* hall.

In 1939 a brand new school was built in North Lane. It included six classrooms, a hall, and cloakrooms to accommodate 240 pupils. When it opened in September 1939 there were 172 children on the roll.

This is not the end of the story of the old church school. It was called into service in 1949, when the North Lane School itself became overcrowded with 314 children on the roll. Two classrooms were brought back into use — a temporary measure that was to last for ten years!

Eventually new classrooms were built at North Lane in November 1960, and the classes at the old Church School finally ceased for ever. The original building is now The Rustington Church Hall.

## Methodist Church Beginnings

On the death of the village blacksmith, his old 'smithy' at the corner of The Street and Broadmark Lane became empty and derelict for several years. A new blacksmith shop opened in Broadmark Lane, on the junction of what is now Bushby Avenue.

In 1875 a small group of Methodists began to worship together in a small cottage (now demolished) called Hedgerville in Broadmark Lane. This was the home of Charles and Louisa Hedger and William and Elizabeth Gates.Within two years this small group had raised sufficient money to buy the 'old smithy'.

Snewin's, builders from Littlehampton, converted the smithy into a chapel. The annexe, which at one time had housed the parish church Sunday School, became a Sunday School for the Methodists. Snewin's made five memorial stones, as well as 'dressing up the chapel on Easter Monday 1878, for a tea party, on the opening of the chapel'.

The membership of the Primitive Methodist Chapel grew quickly from the days of the early pioneers and a new church building became a necessity. The chapel was also a traffic hazard, as it stood well out into a busy main road.

The Summers family donated land in Claigmar Road to the Methodists. A building permit was granted, and the new Methodist church was then built. On 29 May 1952, the congregation held a brief farewell service in the old Primitive Chapel. They then walked the few hundred yards to the new church for a service of thanksgiving, which was conducted by the Rev. Dr. W.E. Sangster.

A small part of the old chapel was preserved, however, when one of the original five memorial stones, dated 1878, that had been laid by a Mrs. Mason, was set into the present building.

## Distinctive Properties Past and Present

Mewsbrook House was built in 1870 by Robert Bushby of Littlehampton for Mrs. Louis Barnes. It was a large castellated building, with extensive grounds, and stood just west of the Mewsbrook swamp on Sea Road, at this period within the boundary of Rustington. The Barnes family occasionally hosted parties in their house and grounds for inmates of the East Preston Union Workhouse, also known as North View and locally as 'The Spike'.

Mrs. Bland purchased Mewsbrook House in 1923-4, and had the building extended in the same eccentric style. She then opened it as a modern hotel, calling it the *Rustington Towers Hotel*. Unfortunately, most of the hotel was destroyed by fire in 1935. There were plans to rebuild it, but they had to be shelved, as findings from test bores taken on the site showed running blue river mud at a depth of 30 feet. The idea of rebuilding was abandoned and the small section of the old hotel that had escaped the fire was demolished. Part of the overgrown garden can still be seen behind the pumping station, including a giant mulberry tree.

In 1894, a large area of land along the Sea Road, west of the Mewsbrooks, was bought by Sir Henry Harben of Warnham. He employed the architect Frederick Wheeler in 1897 to design a convalescent home. It was to have its own concert hall, electricity supply, steam laundry, bacterial drainage treatment system, home farm, and a lodge on a 17½-acre site. So Sir Henry Harben, who was Master of The Worshipful Company of Carpenters, was the founder of one of the most complete convalescent homes of its kind. It is the largest building in the district and, from all points of view, one of the finest. After the outbreak of the Second World War, the home was closed. It was suggested that it should be used as a military hospital, but this was considered inadvisable, owing to the possible danger of the district being in the direct line of an invasion. It re-opened as a convalescent home during the summer of 1948, and has recently celebrated its centenary.

Further eastwards along the sea front, where the Overstrand Estate now stands, was the Millfield Convalescent Home. The five-and-a-half-acre site was bought by the Metropolitan Asylums Board in 1903. Four large buildings were opened as a seaside home for children on 6 April 1904. Later it was taken over by the London County Council, when it became a convalescent home for children suffering from tuberculosis. Dr. Last of Littlehampton was the appointed doctor at the home, which he visited daily. He also played the part of Father Christmas annually for the children. The home was closed and requisitioned by the military at the beginning of the Second World

War. It was left in a derelict state and was not to be used again. In 1958 it was demolished.

However, its final moment of glory was when it was used as one of the timing points in attempts on the world air-speed records. The first, on 7 September 1946 by Group Captain E.M. Donaldson, flying a Gloster Meteor IV, achieved a speed of 615.78 mph, breaking the previous record that had stood at 606.38 mph. The second occasion was on 7 September 1953, when Squadron Leader Neville Duke, OBE, DSO, DFC with two bars and AFC, broke the record again, in a Hawker Hunter mkIII at an average speed of just over 727 mph.

In 1996, to celebrate these two achievements and 50 years to the day after the first record, Rustington Parish Council arranged a suitable ceremony. The special guest, Squadron Leader Neville Duke, unveiled the commemorative plaque, and an invited audience and a large crowd gathered on the sea shore to watch the unveiling. This was followed by a flying display by Capt. S. Hodgkins in a Gloster Meteor and Capt. Brian Henwood in a Hawker Hunter, planes similar to those which broke the records over the original course.

A little further eastwards from this point towards Broadmark Lane is Princess Marina House, earlier known as the Newton Driver Services Club. This was opened in April 1947 by H.R.H. The Duke of Edinburgh, when many Rustington folk turned out to welcome him to the village. The club was founded by Mrs. Newton Driver, O.B.E., in memory of her husband, for the use of officers of the Royal Navy, the Army and the Royal Air Force. The name was changed to Princess Marina House when the Princess visited the club in 1962. It became a home for ex-RAF personnel in 1969, when the complex was taken over by the RAF Benevolent Fund.

Many people born in the years between 1946-79, whose parents lived between Bognor Regis and Worthing, may be surprised to learn from birth certificates, that they were born in Rustington. This is because The Zachary Merton Maternity Hospital in Rustington covered this catchment area.

The name Zachary Merton is that of a generous philanthropist. He left a large sum of money, on the death of his wife, to be used for the founding of convalescent homes, and Rustington was the site of one of these homes. The architects were Messrs. Stanley Hall, Easton and Robertson of London, and it was built, at a cost of £32,896 by Messrs. Chapman, Lowry and Puttick of Haslemere, as a convalescent home for mothers, babies and their toddlers, and was opened on 28 April 1937.

Later, it became a maternity hospital and held an enviable reputation for over 30 years. Eventually it was scaled down and finally closed as a maternity unit in June 1979. The building re-opened in November of that same year as a community hospital.

During 1936, 'The Lido', a first-class holiday complex, was established in the village. It possessed a ballroom, lecture/conference hall, floodlit swimming pool, children's pool, outdoor roller skating rink, bowling greens, and tennis courts, to name a few of the amenities. This was all set in 40 acres of ground, with flower gardens and coloured fountains. *The Lido*, however, did not hold a licence to sell alcoholic drinks, which was catered for at the adjacent *Broadmark Hotel*, built for the owner Mr. Sydney Jones at the same time.

During the 1939-45 War, like all other large properties in Rustington, The Lido and the *Broadmark Hotel* were requisitioned by the military. On the run-up to D-Day on 6 June 1944, thousands of Americans troops arrived in this country to take part in this momentous operation. Mr. Rockall, the local troop billeting officer, was asked to prepare the whole complex to house the first troops to arrive. While the American troops were stationed there, in 1943 they gave a large Christmas party for the children of servicemen in the village.

After the war, in 1947 The Lido was sold to the Workers Travel Association (W.T.A.). Ten years later it was renamed Mallon Dene, after Sir J. J. Mallon, head of the W.T.A. The holiday complex was eventually demolished in 1968, and the site is now occupied by the Mallon Dene Estate. The *Broadmark Hotel* continued in use until 1984, when that also was demolished, and the 'Broadmark Beach' flats now occupy this site.

Lying almost opposite the old Pigeon House Lane, that is, next to West Preston Manor, there once stood a fine old flint building called Walnut Tree Cottage. Documents appertaining to it, dating from 1615, revealed that in the early 18th century it was an inn, known by its sign as the *New Inn*. (The sign in those days was a brush or branch of a tree, tied on a pole above the inn door, an elementary form of today's inn signs.) This was probably the first ale house in Rustington. It was reputedly the meeting place of the Rustington band of smugglers known as 'The Ragman Totts':

> A few days since, Messrs. Heaseman and Roberts, revenue officers at Rustington, seized from the Ragman Totts company of smugglers, 49 casks of cognac, brandy and geneva, and lodged the same in the Arundel Custom House. 5 Nov. 1787.

After the *New Inn* ceased trading in 1829 it was sold, and became a family home once again, named Walnut Tree Cottage. Finally West Sussex County Council bought it in 1949 for £1,050. Being in a bad state of repair by then, it was demolished soon after for road improvements.

Rustington now has three public houses, namely the *Windmill Inn*, the *Fletcher Arms* and the *Lamb Inn*. The *Windmill Inn* to the north east of the village derives its name from the mill that stood opposite it. The licence was transferred from the *New Inn* in Station Road when it closed in 1829. A new *Windmill Inn* was purpose-built in 1909, replacing the original *Windmill Inn*. The old inn was converted into two cottages, known as Windmill Cottages 1 and 2 and the new inn stands just south of the old inn. The walls of its old bowling alley can still be seen in the garden of the cottages.

The *Fletcher Arms*, standing near Angmering Station, was converted from a house called Munmere Cottage, where J. Warr(en) a fly proprietor lived and at one time had his livery stables. In 1933 the cottage was extended and converted into a public house by Messrs. Henty and Constable. It was named *The Fletcher Arms* after Sir Henry Aubrey Fletcher of Ham Manor. The inn licence was not new but was transferred from the *Red Lion Inn* at Angmering village. Mr. and Mrs. M.H. Thomas opened the premises for business in February 1934, and the pub remained in the hands of the Thomas family for 44 years.

The *Lamb Inn*, standing opposite the parish church, could be a contender for the first pub in the village. It is not clear from existing records whether it was opened in 1779 or 1809, but we think 1809 is more likely, when James Richardson the owner took out an extra mortgage of £400. He was also a cordwainer, combining the two trades to make ends meet. Documents of 1779 refer to a cellar in the building, so perhaps the inn was already in existence then. Would an old cottage *c*.1660 have had a cellar? This inn was also used as the local early type of bank, a venue for land and property auctions, and the home of the Sunday School.

The old *Lamb Inn* was a long, low single-storey building, which was demolished and replaced by a new purpose-built inn during 1902. This had a large adjoining hall, which was used for various functions, including smoking concerts, wedding receptions, The Ancient Order of Foresters' meetings, school classes and occasionally as a mortuary. Later it was used for billiards and snooker, and it had three full-size tables. The hall was pulled down in 1959 for road widening, which incidentally never materialised. The *Lamb Inn* has undergone many modernisations since then.

*    *    *

It comes as a surprise to many people to learn that there was an air station in Rustington during the First World War; it was, in fact, an American aerodrome. Building only began in 1917, one year before the end of the war, so it never had time to become fully operational. However, aircraft used it for flying in spares and equipment. Over 40 per cent of the projects were complete by early 1918. It was to have been the base for American personnel to train on the Handley Page 0/400, a night bomber with a 100ft. wing span, before leaving for active service in France. The grass runway ran from north to south, so that aircraft could take off towards the sea. The main entrance to the airfield was from Station Road, now the entrance to Sea Avenue (Sea Estate). The airfield had its own railway siding, a branch line off the main south-coast railway that ran between Brighton and Portsmouth. The line served the mess and barracks as well as the airfield and crossed Station Road near Sea Avenue.

Only two airfield buildings remain in situ: 'Fairholme', a bungalow converted from the guard house, at the entrance to Sea Avenue; and 'Nortons'/'Galleons', a bungalow from a converted salvage shed, in Preston Avenue. The arrival of so many American and Canadian troops to work on the aerodrome must have had a considerable impact on the quiet, sleepy village life in Rustington.

Apart from the war years, building development within the parish has never ceased, and the population has grown to over 12,500 from 616 in 1901.

Rustington is still primarily a residential area, favoured by young and old alike. It retains its old-world cottages, to which have been added bungalows, modern blocks of flats, as well as a superb shopping centre. Despite extensive development, it still has its former charm and jealously guards its special village identity.

**1** Pigeon House Farm before it was renovated in 1946, by Mr. F. Mariner. This is the only remaining timber-framed, jettied house in the village. Previously known as 'Old Farm', it belonged to the West Preston Manor Estate. It was reputedly haunted according to the Henson family, who lived there between 1860-70. Mr. Henson was farm bailiff to Mr. Thomas Bushby.

**2** West Preston Manor showing the south elevation of the house during Mr. Thomas Bushbys occupation. Mr. Bushby was a principal land-owner, auctioneer and farmer. He died in 1915, without male issue, aged 88. The Bushbys held the manor from 1777 until 1933, when it was sold. It then became a school.

**3** *(left)*  Mr. Thomas Bushby watches while his men are sheep shearing in one of his barns on the manor.

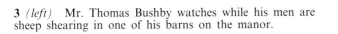

**4** *(below left)*  The Shepherd, together with a flock of his sheep, on West Preston Manor Farm.

**5** *(below)*  Mr. Richard Henson poses by his steam plough tackle, while his sons Noah and James carry on working with the other farm labourers.

**6** Richard Henson's hay wagon with a traction engine hard at work in the hay fields.

**7** In 1765 The Duke of Richmond acquired The Manor of Rustington and he had maps and schedules made of the village. Herne Farm appears on these maps. Herne/Heron possibly derives its name from the Old English *hyrne* — i.e. land in a corner or angle. An early picture when the Boons were the farmers.

**8**  Allangate Dairy Farm, Station Road. These two delightful ponies were used to advertise the dairy products.

**9**  Rustington Manor House. Probably Rustington's oldest house, it became dilapidated as time went by. It then became the home of farm labourers, rather than the tenant farmer for the lord of the manor. It was bought in 1919, and restored to something like its former medieval grace, by the new owner, Count Albert Gustave de Belleroche. This picture shows farm labourer William Gates 'Shep' leaning over the flint wall *c.*1900.

**10** *(left)* Quaker Smith's Farm, *c.*1890. All that now remains of this farm is the cottage on the left known as Church Farm Cottage (rear view). The farmyard has been used as a builder's yard for many years, both by C.J. Drake and Hall & Co. A small parade of shops occupies the site of the old barns.

**11** *(below left)* Cudlow Farm. This 1899 picture shows Dorothy Cobden carrying her younger brother, Richard, standing in the doorway of their father's farmhouse. Her father was cousin of Richard Cobden, of Corn Law fame. They took over the farm from the Newman family in 1862. The house and barn are still in existence, although Cudlow Avenue was cut through the farmyard in 1930.

**12** *(below)* Hobbs Farm, *c.*1900. The entrance gates to the farm are on the left of this picture. The house dates from 1690. Roger and Elizabeth Barwick had it built to replace an existing house. Elizabeth Barwick inherited the land and property from her father John Upperton. The farm takes its name from the Hobbs family who were the owners in the 18th century. Cudlow Farm and barns can be seen on the right.

**13** 'Shep' Gates with horses 'Punch' and 'Flower', ploughing in the Shaftesbury fields. In the background, the roof of Mr. Thomas Summers' house, Normanhurst, can be seen.

**14** Mr. Thomas Summers (1851-1933), property developer and land-owner, lived at Normanhurst, Broadmark Lane (house now demolished). He built the Glenville, Waverley, and Claigmar Road houses and also Shaftesbury House. He built the Broadway mansions in 1909; now 'Alldays' stands on this site.

**15**  Mr. Summers had Crown permission to collect a certain amount of sand and shingle from the beach on payment of royalty. These materials went through a salt removing process, before they were used in house building. In this picture, Punch and Flower are at work again.

**16**  Reaping time in The Seafield, The Sea Mill and Millfield Convalescent Home can be seen in the background. Guess who is at work, *c*.1910?

**17** Victoria Cottage, *c*.1890. Later called 'The Anchorage', the house was built in 1880 for The Victoria Brick and Tile Co. by Robert Bushby, in the Norman Shaw style. It was the home of Mr. and Mrs. Shepherd and their nine sons. He was manager for John Eede Butt, who later owned the brick fields. The house was demolished to make way for Artex Avenue industrial estate in 1962.

**18** Brick fields. The only known photograph of John Eede Butt's site near A.B.C. corner, Worthing Road. Victoria Cottage can be seen in the middle background.

**19** Mr. Linfield's brickworks in Worthing/Albert Roads.

**20** Albert Road, *c*.1929. Brickmakers' cottages. The gas holder and the gas company house have both now gone.

**21** Worthing Road, *c*.1916, when two local children could safely stand in the middle of the road. The picture also shows a row of Mr. Linfield's brick field cottages.

**22** Wedding, 13 April 1912. Outside Ham View, on the corner of Worthing and Albert Roads, stands the bridegroom, Albert George Barnes and his bride, Harriet Lily (née Hope).

**23** *(left)* London, Brighton & South Coast Railway. The attractive waiting room and signal box on the down line at Angmering Station, *c.*1908.

**24** *(below left)* Angmering Station *c.*1912 shows six of the regular staff. (From left to right) Ted Leggat, clerk / porter, George Leggat, clerk / porter, Bill Thorpe, signalman, Fred Lucas, porter, Billy Moon, porter, Horace Hayward, Station Master.

**25** *(below)* The Hoover Express pulling away from Angmering Station. A convention had been held at The Lido in Rustington, 1938. (Courtesy of Middleton Press.)

**26** The first village shop, bought by John Simpson (the sitting tenant) from Geo. Cortis in 1841. He had a bakery and sold grocery and provisions. Mary Ann Humphrey bought the shop in 1884 from James Simpson, son of John, for £500. Photo *c*.1910.

**27** The postmen: (from left to right) Bill Edmunds, Mr. Corney, Jack Greysmark and Jack MacDonald, *c*.1905. The mail was sorted and then delivered from Angmering Station, which had its own postmark.

**28** Charles James Drake, property developer, with his wife Leopoldine and children, photographed by Mr. Edwin Allen of Church Road. He was responsible for many of the pictures that survive today. Mr. Drake married Leopoldine Chatfield, daughter of the local wheelwright, at the parish church on 5 June 1876. Mr. Drake built the 'new' *Lamb Inn* in 1902.

**29** The *Lamb Inn*. The concert hall that later became a billiard saloon. The hall was demolished for road widening in 1956, and the *Lamb Inn* was also modernised at this time.

**30** Dingley Nursery, Christmas Day 1951. Jack Kessler, owner, is seen watering some of the plants at his nursery in Old Manor Road. Very few nursery pictures now exist.

**31** Smuggler's Nursery, Holmes Lane, advert drawn by Charles Hunnibal, Mrs. Manning's brother, showing some of the layout of the nursery. Mr. Manning was the owner from November 1947 to its closure in 1964. Chanctonbury and part of Cove Road now run through the site.

**32** Sea Mill, 1910, showing a rough unmade Sea Road at its junction with Sea Lane. A great storm on the night of 5 March 1912 badly damaged the mill, and it was never to work again. It was demolished the following year. The Millfield Convalescent Home can be seen left background.

**33** Windmill corner, Mill Lane, *c*.1890, showing Humphrey's Mill, so called because it was owned and worked by James Humphrey and his son Peter for many years. The miller's house and cottage, adjoining the mill, were built *c*.1827. The original 17th-century miller's cottage, on the east side of the road, was converted into the first *Windmill Inn* at this time. The existing *Windmill Inn* was built in 1909. The miller's house was demolished *c*.1960; the adjoining 'new' miller's cottage is still there but much rebuilt. The windmill itself was taken down in 1896.

**34** Rustington's third mill. For a few years, opposite the Sea Mill, stood a timber tripod post-mill. It was taken down in 1857, loaded onto a trailer and transported via Arundel to Fishbourne, where it ended its days. This picture shows it at Fishbourne. Below is a report in the *Brighton Gazette*, 5 October 1848, of the transportation of Rustington's 'third mill' from Angmering to its site off Sea Lane.

A windmill belonging to Mr. Graves Bailey was last week successfully removed, in an erect position, from near the residence of Mr. Gratwicke, at Angmering, to the sea-side at Rustington, a distance of two miles; and, as may be supposed, so extraordinary an object on the turnpike road, especially while on the viaduct over the railway, attracted crowds of spectators. The removal was accomplished by the following means:- A very strong frame work, or 'undercarriage,' of timber, upon four extremely broad solid wheels, was introduced beneath the horizontal timbers supporting the main-post and the spurs of the mill, and between the brickwork pier upon which the whole rested; the weight was then, by the aid of wedges and powerful screws, transmitted from the piers to the carriage, to which horses, varying along the way in number from nineteen to twenty-four, were attached, and after this manner the removal was accomplished with comparatively little difficulty. Extensive lopping of the trees had to be made along the greater part of the route.

**35** *(left)*   Rustington parish church in 1854. This picture was taken by Dr. Diamond before the church restoration took place. Here we see the old five-barred gate that served as the entrance to the churchyard. The lych-gate that stands here today was erected in 1860, using old roof timbers from the church.

**36** *(below left)*   Church interior in 1854, looking east, showing the old box pews and the east windows when they still contained clear glass. This picture was taken by Dr. Diamond.

**37** *(below)*   Church interior, *c.*1905, showing oil lamp lighting, new pews and stained glass. The chancel arch with embellishment, carried out under the direction of Mr. N.J. Comper, depicts the Ten Commandments. (*Parish Magazine*, May 1941.)

**38** Church interior 1939/45. Wartime black-out curtains are draped either side of the east window, a necessary precaution at that period.

**39** Rustington Parish Church, *c.*1890. Children gather for some occasion outside the west gate. The ancient elm tree (left) stood by a stile, where a footpath led to Worthing Road and Bridge Mill. Church Road was built here in 1897.

**40** Rustington National School, built 1859, on part of the Rev. H.J. Rush's land. He gave the school, which accommodated 63 pupils, and the land on which it stood to the parish of Rustington. The Rev. Rush was vicar of Rustington 1858-1871.

41    School children, *c*.1897, at the Rustington National School.

42    School children, *c*.1899. In costume, ready for one of the school plays, put on to raise money for the school enlargement. Dorothy Cobden of Cudlow Farm is the little shepherdess with the crook, on the right of the picture.

**43** Group 3, school children, *c.*1918. Back row (left to right) Harry Manley, Doris Cheeseman, Leslie Lee, Bernice Henson, Leslie Hills, and Stanley Hills; (centre row) Alfonso White, Dorothy Cornwall, Cecil Wilmer, Agnes Lidbetter, Jim Betts, Dorothy Kilhams, Tommy Manley; (front row) Bert Henson, George Weller, Marjorie Fuller, Leslie Sullivan, Winnie Dormand, and ?.

**44** New council school. North Lane School was built in 1939 at a cost of £12,000.

**45** North Lane School, showing the classrooms and corridor of the new school.

**46** Hedgerville, Broadmark Lane, the home of Charles and Louisa Hedger. Louisa ran a small school for local children here, before the National School opened in 1859. In the late 1860s William and Elizabeth Gates went to live with them, and it was here that the first meeting of the Methodists took place. In 1878 they moved to the vacant 'old blacksmith's forge' in The Street.

**47** Primitive Methodist Chapel, converted and enlarged from the old smithy. It was opened in 1878. The Methodists moved to their present church when the old chapel had to be demolished in October 1952 to make way for the new shopping parade to be built there. Behind the chapel can be seen the trees that surrounded Clock House/White House Field. Local garden and church fêtes were held here. Today it is the site of Sterling Parade.

**48** Methodist Sunday school children *c*.1910, outside the chapel. Back row (boys) left to right, George Woolven, Percy Hale, Fred Gates, Claude Gates, Eddie Woolven, Sidney Gates; centre row (girls) left to right, Rose Gates, Nellie Parsons, Pansy Woolven, May Mills, Dorothy Yeates, Gwen Bailey, Marjorie Hale; front row left to right, Alfred Lidbetter, Agnes Lidbetter, Eddie Woolven, Nellie Gates and Reginald Gates.

**49** Blacksmith shop on the corner of Bushby Avenue and Broadmark Lane which replaced the 'old' smithy taken over by the Methodists. Two blacksmiths were known to work here, Jimmy Francis followed by Mr. Hubbard. Mr. Hubbard was noted for the pet parrot that kept him company.

**50** *Rustington Towers Hotel*, converted from Mewsbrook House that was built in 1870 by Robert Bushby for Mr. Louis Barnes. Mrs. Bland in 1924 had it extended and enlarged and opened it as *The Rustington Towers Hotel*.

**51** Site preparation and well-boring for the Rustington Convalescent Home, 1896.

**52** Opening ceremony programme, when the Right Rev. The Lord Bishop of Chichester opened the Rustington Convalescent Home on 20 March 1897.

**53** Rustington Convalescent Home, *c.*1905. Note the pony and trap transport.

**54** Patients, *c*.1912. Some of the men who came to convalesce at Rustington. The donkey and cart had to get in the act, of course.

**55** Transport, pony fashion, *c*.1913, one of the means of transport between the home and the station. Note the rough surface of Sea Road, which was not made up until the 1930s. I trust the trap was well sprung!

**56** Sir Henry Harben, founder of the Rustington Convalescent Home that opened in 1897, is pictured standing outside the main entrance to the home.

**57** Miss Beatrice Sharp was matron between 1913 and 1919. The photo was taken by Edwin Allen of Church Road, Rustington. He was responsible for many of the local postcards.

**58** *(top right)* Millfield Convalescent Home, 1903. Men at work, building the home. Note the large work force, and the wooden scaffolding, which was roped together. It opened as a sunshine home for children.

**59** *(right)* Millfield Convalescent Home, 1903-58. It occupied 5½ acres of land north of the old Sea Mill. It could accommodate 100 patients in its four large wings. It was requisitioned during 1939/45 war by the military, and was left derelict and demolished in 1958.

**60** World air speed records. Neville Duke OBE, DSO, DFC and two bars, AFC, unveiling a commemorative plaque celebrating the 50th anniversary of the record set up by Group Capt. Donaldson DSO, AFC in a Gloster Meteor in 1946, and a new world air speed record set up Neville Duke himself in a Hawker Hunter in 1953. The course timing markers for the record were on the coast between Sea Lane, Rustington, where the plaque was unveiled, and Kingston. [Photo courtesy of Beckett newspapers]

**61** Newton Driver Services Club. The opening ceremony was performed by HRH Prince Philip on 23 April 1949. (Now called The Princess Marina Home.)

**62** HRH Prince Philip talks to the officer in charge of the local Sea Cadets, during their inspection, at the opening ceremony of the Newton Driver Services Club.

**63** Zachary Merton in 1938; a convalescent home for mothers and their babies, before it became a maternity hospital.

**64** *Broadmark Hotel*, built for Sydney Jones in 1936, showing the south frontage. It held a full licence unlike the adjoining Lido, which was unlicensed. It was demolished in 1984.

**65** *Broadmark Hotel* showing the north side, the front entrance and car park, *c.*1937.

**66** Programme and menu for the opening dinner dance and cabaret, 22 May 1936. It contains the signatures of Sydney Jones and other prominent guests.

**67** The Lido holiday camp opened in 1936 with a dinner dance. This photo shows the dining room before the first guests arrived and the waitresses are standing by. The Lido could accommodate 450 guests and 50 staff and had 236 bedrooms.

**68** Swimming pools at The Lido holiday camp which later became The Mallon Dene. The whole complex was demolished in 1968 and is now the site of the Mallon Dene Estate off Broadmark Lane.

**69** Physical culture was one of the features at the Lido; there were many sports and games facilities available for the guests.

**70** Mallon Dene. The Lido was renamed when the W.T.A. (Workers Travel Association), whose chairman was Sir J.J. Mallon, took it over in 1948.

**71** *The New Inn*, possibly Rustington's first beer house, 1778-1829, owned by James Burfield. It was sited opposite West Preston Manor. The original cottage was let in 1615 to John Hebenden, a blacksmith, at a rent of one peppercorn for a term of 10,000 years. Bought by Margaret Bushby in 1829, it reverted to a cottage (Walnut Tree). Eventually in 1949 it was bought for £1,050 by West Sussex County Council and it was then demolished for road widening.

**72** The 'old' *Windmill Inn*, with its adjoining bakery, at the foot of windmill bridge. Part of this building was the original miller's cottage *c.*1613. A new purpose-built inn was erected south of the cottage in 1909 and the old inn was converted into two cottages that are still there today. The licence was probably transferred in 1829, when Thomas Humphrey moved from the *New Inn* to the *Windmill Inn*. He was landlord for George Constable (brewers), the new owner.

**73** The 'new' *Windmill Inn* was built in 1909 in Mill Lane, where mine host was Herbert Ralph Booker.

**74** Munmere Cottage was named after the lake that was here until the railway came, when it was partially filled in. Mr. Warren (Warr), the fly proprietor, lived here. Munmere Cottage was converted into *The Fletcher Arms* in 1936 by Messrs. Henty and Constable.

**75** *The Fletcher Arms*. When it first opened in 1936, Mr. H. Thomas was licensee, and it remained in the Thomas family until 1977, when Mr. and Mrs. Peter Thomas retired.

**76** The 'old' *Lamb Inn*. The Stoner family, licensees between 1890 and 1910, stand outside the single-storey building of the original *Lamb Inn*.

**77** Children at play outside the 'old' *Lamb Inn* when it was safe to do so.

**78** The 'old' *Lamb Inn* and cottage. This picture shows the inn keeper's house, demolished in 1900, adjoining the *Lamb Inn,* which was subsequently demolished in 1901. The cottage on the right was called Rose Cottage, which suffered a similar fate. It was to become a car park for the 'new' *Lamb Inn.*

**79** Hackney carriages (Model 'T' Fords) for hire outside the 'new' *Lamb Inn,* built in 1902 by C.J. Drake. Percy Hale, a barman at the *Lamb Inn,* was the driver of the car on the left and John Woolven was the other driver.

**80** Smoking concert. One of the concerts held at the Lamb Inn Hall before it became a billiard hall, *c.*1914/8. The hall was also used on occasions as a mortuary.

**81** Rustington's aerodrome. In 1918 the Americans were building an aerodrome for the Handley Page 0/400 night bomber. This is now the site of the Sea Estate. The plan, taken from a micro film, is reproduced by kind permission of The National Archives of the United States, Washington, and shows the development of the site in detail.

| | | |
|---|---|---|
| 1A AERO SHED | 12 GUNNERY WORKSHOP | 32/A REGIMENTAL STORE |
| 1B AERO SHED TWIN | 13 PHOTOGRAPHY HUT | 33A-K BARRACK BLOCKS |
| 1C AERO SHLD TWIN | 14 WIRELESS & BOMB HUT | 34A-C BATH HOUSES |
| 1D AERO SHED | 15 BUZZING & PICTURE HUT | 35A-D LATRINES/ABLUTIONS |
| 2 A.R.S. SHED | 16A-E FLIGHT GROUP COMMANDERS- | 36A-C DRYING ROOMS |
| 3A PLANE STORE | 17 DEPOT OFFICE          OFFICES | 37/A COAL YARD |
| 3B PLANE STORE | 18 GUARD HOUSE | 38 RECEPTION STATION |
| 4 SALVAGE SHED | 19/A LATRINES | 40 LATRINE |
| 5 TECHNICAL STORE | 20 BOMB DROP TOWER | 41 MACHINE GUN RANGE |
| 6 POWER HOUSE | 23 PETROL STORE AERO | 42 COMPASS PLATFORM |
| 6A POWER HOUSE ADDITION | 24 OFFICERS MESS | 43/A PETROL FILLING POINT |
| 7 WORKSHOP WOOD | 25A/B STAFF OFFICERS HUTS | 44 MAP READING HUT |
| 8 WORKSHOP METAL | 26A-D PUPIL OFFICERS HUTS | 45A-C PETROL STORAGE TANKS |
| 8A WORKSHOP METAL | 27 LATRINE STAFF | 46 PETROL PUMP HOUSE |
| 9A MOTOR TRANSPORT | 28 LATRINE PUPILS | 47 TOWER |
| 9B MOTOR TRANSPORT | 29 SERGEANTS MESS | 48 MORTUARY |
| 10 GENERAL LECTURE HUT | 30/A LATRINE SERGEANTS | 49 WATER PUMP HOUSE |
| 11 GUNNERY INSTRUCTION HUT | 31 REGIMENTAL MESS | 50 RAILWAY BRANCH LINE |

Rustington Handley Page Aerodrome

AMERICAN AIRFORCE TRAINING DEPOT 1918

SITE PLAN

**82** The Handley Page 0/400 night bomber had a 100ft wingspan. This photo was taken from the microfilm.

**83** Sea View Café, at the corner of Hendon Avenue and Sea Road, was used as a canteen for troops during the Second World War.

**84** Sea View canteen. Troops of the 8th Batt. Royal Welsh Fusiliers, D. Coy, 17th Platoon stationed at Millfield Convalescent Home, here pictured outside the canteen in 1941.

**85** The LDVs' unofficial transport, supplied by Jimmy Piggott and his pony Bimbo, outside the village hall. This was the headquarters of the Local Defence Volunteers.

**86** 'Dads' Army'. The official transport of the LDV, moving off for rifle practice at the Arundel rifle range. A warning notice on the trailer reads 'tighten wheel nuts'.

**87** Home Guard beach patrol off Broadmark; Corporal Fred Gates is on the right.

**88** The War Memorial, unveiled on 6 July 1952 by Admiral C. Caslon, CB, CBE, RN, to commemorate those who gave their lives in the two world wars 1914/18 and 1939/45.

**89** Ceremonial order of service for the unveiling of the Rustington village war memorial, held on the corner of The Street and Claigmar Road, 6 July 1952.

## Rustington
## Village War Memorial

This Memorial, which bears the names of those people of Rustington who gave their lives in the two Wars 1914-1918 and 1939-1945, is now to be unveiled in the presence of representatives of all sections of the Village community this sixth day of July, 1952.

**LIVE THOU FOR ENGLAND
WE FOR ENGLAND DIED**

## CEREMONIAL

———

HYMN (A.M. No. 165): Oh, God, our Help in ages past. (Led by Choir)

PRAYER

BIBLE READING: Wisdom of Solomon, Chap. 3, verses 1-9

SPEECH OF INTRODUCTION BY CHAIRMAN

SPEECH AND UNVEILING BY ADMIRAL C. CASLON, C.B., C.B.E., R.N.

LAYING OF WREATH BY REPRESENTATIVE BODIES

LAST POST (Standards " DIP ")

SHORT SILENCE

REVEILLE (Standards " CARRY ")

NATIONAL ANTHEM. (Led by Choir)

**90** The Village Memorial Hall, Woodlands Avenue, headquarters of the Home Guard. When the H.G. were disbanded after the war, they donated a drinking water fountain to the village. It can be seen on the left of the picture, inside the gate. Unfortunately it was vandalised and never replaced.

**91** Almshouses in Station Road, adjacent to East Preston church (note the stone spire). These cottages were given to the parish by a lady benefactor, *c.*1700, and tied up with The Ashley Trust of 1698. When the East Preston Union Workhouse was built to cater for the needs of the poor in the area, the cottages were no longer required. They were purchased at auction by Mr. R.A. Warren of East Preston in 1870 and remained in private use until they were demolished in 1931.

**92**  Floods in Station Road, close to West Preston Manor, *c*.1917.

**93** *Shirlands Hotel.* This single-storey hotel and club started life as the depot office for the American airbase in Rustington in the 1914/18 war. It was situated on the eastern corner of the main entrance to the airfield, now the entrance to Sea Avenue. It was demolished *c.*1965, and Shirlands Court was built on this site.

**94** Station Road, when elm trees lined the road before Dutch elm disease struck with such devastation in the village. This 1950 photograph illustrates just how quiet and peaceful Rustington was in those days.

**95** Woodbine Cottage at the junction of Mill Lane, Station Road and Ash Lane. It has a well-worn date plaque showing 1793. The right wing was built by C.J. Drake in 1910 for the then owner, Mrs. Faulkner. It was at one time used as tea rooms.

**96** Ash Lane looking north *c*.1920, before horse-less carriages were much in evidence. To the right, in the grass verge, can be seen a wooden bench. Strangely there is a wooden seat in the same position today. On the left you can glimpse the roof of Whitecroft with Church Farm Nursery just beyond.

**97** Whitecroft, built in 1903, was originally known as Church Farm Bungalow. This was Rustington's first butcher's shop, which also had a dairy. The business, however, was not successful. Subsequently it was sold, and renamed Whitecroft by the new owners, the Buchanans. It was requisitioned by Canadian troops during the 1939/45 war. At one time the parish council considered buying Whitecroft for a village centre, but the idea was rejected. Church Farm Estate is now on this site.

**98** The village 'bobby' in 1908. The parish council thought it expedient to have a police constable stationed in the village. Here we see him outside Mrs. Upfield's grocery shop in Ash Lane.

**99** Ash Lane in the 1920s. On the left is Stonefield Bakery, built by C.J. Drake and run by the Booker family. Wilmer's the grocers and Rita's the drapers adjoin on the right.

**100** Westminster Bank was the first bank to open for business in Rustington, in 1935. It was alongside Welling's the estate agent, in a room of the old house called The Matthew's and it stood opposite the junction of The Street and Ash Lane, now part of Broadmark Parade. The Bank opened for several hours each week.

**101**  Ash Lane in 1921, showing the road junction with the old finger post pointing down The Street to Bognor and Littlehampton. The Matthew's, then a private house, can be seen on the right.

**102**  Ash Lane, 1955. The same position as No.101, with The Matthew's long since gone, and Broadmark Parade shops, built in 1937, in its place. Due to the onset of the 1939/45 war, few of the shops were completed or open for business during the war.

**103** Broadmark Lane in 1921, looking south. Showing the finger post, and the Matthew's extreme left, with the roof of Broadmark Cottage beyond. Many people will remember this cottage when it was Marters Market Gardens shop, as it only closed in 1970. This area is now occupied by Somerfield Supermarket.

**104** Broadmark Cottage, *c.*1903, pictured by Edwin Allen, showing the Knight family who were living here at the time. Edward, the youngest of the children, born in 1902, is in Mrs. Knight's arms. His father, Mr. Herbert Knight, was parish clerk.

**105** Bumble Cottage, *c.*1920. This little thatched cottage was built in 1878 on the corner of Bushby Avenue and Broadmark Lane.

**106** Bushby Avenue as it looked in the 1920s. It derived its name from the land-owner, Thomas Bushby of West Preston manor.

**107** Glenville Road in the early 1900s, showing a Rustington Dairies milk cart, drawn by a pony, on their village round.

**108** Waverley Road, June 1910, when fire broke out in Mr. Summers' (builder's) workshop, which adjoined the terrace of houses. Workmen can be seen removing furniture from the fire to safety.

**109** Rear view of the fire in Waverley Road, where workmen gather round to discuss the calamity. Note the fireman up the ladder on the next door property.

**110**  Holiday bungalows in 1927, at the sea end of Broadmark Lane. A deep ditch running the length of this lane meant that access to these properties was mainly over small wooden bridges. To the right, a pony munches away at the grass.

**111**  Broadmark Lane *c.*1920, viewed from the beach. On the left is the entrance to Seafield Road and on the right is Normanhurst, home of Thomas Summers, the builder and developer. It is said that Mrs. Summers named the roads and houses from books she had read. The origin of 'Claigmar' Road is unknown, but it is understood to be the only one in England.

112 Pile driving in 1938 to erect new breakwaters off Broadmark beach.

113 Sea Road in 1912. This road only came into existence in 1830, and was the responsibility of the Littlehampton Ferry Trustees. It was still in a poor state of repair in the 1930s.

**114** *(left)*  The Mewsbrook swamp in 1935. This was the delta of the river Arun centuries ago. This part of Rustington was taken over by Littlehampton in 1933 and was turned into a boating lake and pleasure garden.

**115** *(below left)*  The creation of the Mewsbrook boating lake. During drainage work a 'dug-out' boat was uncovered, and also possible signs of a Roman harbour.

**116** *(below)*  Sea Road in the 1920s. The high wall on the left was in front of Seafield Court which stood close to the junction of Sea Lane.

**117** Seafield Court in 1959. Lady Armstrong and her family rented the residence for a period during the late 19th century. She had a famous daughter-in-law, Dame Nellie Melba, the prima-donna. The property also served for a time as a school for boys before being demolished in 1964.

**118** Seafield Cottage *c.*1900, at the south-west end of Sea Lane. This was the home of the Gates family, seen here having their photograph taken. Two sisters, their husbands and families shared the cottage. Fitzalan Court stands on the site of the demolished cottage.

**119** 'Been fishing', c.1905. Pictured at the rear of Seafield Cottage (left to right), are William Gates, Alfred Gates, and Sam Salter of Hobbs Farm.

**120** Tea Rooms, 1901-13. The Gates sisters opened the tea room, with only 2s. 6d. [25p] worth of mineral waters to sell. Later they were able to serve tea and cakes, and the business ran very successfully as Rustington's first tea rooms. Pictured left to right are William Gates, Daisy Gates and Mrs. Gates (seated), while Lois Gates feeds the goat.

**121** *(above)*  Scout camp in 1910. The field adjoining Seafield Cottage was used for camping by visiting scout troops during the summer periods. The South Acton scout group are on parade in this photograph.

**122** *(above right)*  South Acton scouts with their hand cart outside Morrallee's newspaper shop, next to Rustington Manor House. The billboard advertises 'Law of the Lawless' at the Electric Palace Cinema, Terminus Road, Littlehampton.

**123** *(right)*  On fatigues at the cook house, the cook was Mr. Tom Chatfield, a local man who took on odd jobs.

**124** Marama, Sea Road. One of the attractive properties that once graced Rustington's seafront. It is said that house parties were given here by J. Arthur Rank for his starlets, including Stewart Grainger and Patricia Roc, but the author has not been able to substantiate this story. The house was demolished in 1976.

**125** Xylophone House, built in 1937 and then called Clist St Mary. Teddy Brown, the famous American xylophonist, renamed it Xylophone House when he bought the property in 1940. Two further owners are recorded, who also changed its name, firstly to Hemmington House and lastly to Bon Accord. In 1976 it suffered the fate of so many fine Rustington properties. Marama Gardens now stands on part of this site.

**126** Brough House was built *c*.1925 for Mr. Agnew-Ansdell, as was the delightful dolls' house, called Virginia Cottage, built in the garden for his children. The whole area was a sheer delight, with temples, grottoes, stone animals and fairy-tale characters, along with the famous elfin oak, carved by the sculptor Ivor Innes. The gardens were opened occasionally to the public and they raised funds for the Littlehampton Cottage Hospital.

**127** Virginia Cottage. The cottage had its own kitchen, sitting room and double bedroom, all fully furnished. Electricity, water and telephone were all connected. After the 1939/45 war it was used as a private residence, the roof having been raised to allow adult access. It was demolished along with Brough House in 1984. The Gilberts now occupy part of this site.

**128** *(left)* Seafield Cottage, showing the entrance to Seafield Court in Sea Lane in 1920. The Pantiles is visible in the left background.

**129** *(below left)* Seafield Road, 1927. The sign-board reads 'Rustington Tennis Courts — open to non residents — 2 persons 1/6d, 4 persons 2/6d — tickets at the Pavilion Tea Rooms'. The houses and cottages then were mainly used as holiday accommodation.

**130** *(below)* Milk cart, 1927. Mr. F.G. Davies stands by his milk float in Seafield Road. The Rustington Dairy was in Broadway Mansions.

**131** Sir Hubert Parry, the composer, stands with his wife, Lady Maude, outside Knights Croft, his home in Sea Lane *c*.1903. He was possibly Rustington's most famous resident, and lived here between 1880 and 1918.

**132** Knights Croft House. Sir Hubert Parry and Lady Maude Parry go for a stroll in the garden. They had two daughters, Dorothea and Gwendoline and Sir Hubert's yacht 'Dolgwandle' was named after them. Knights Croft House was designed by Norman Shaw, and built by Robert Bushby. The decorative tiles in the house were by William de Morgan, the wallpapers by William Morris.

**133** Cudlow House as it appeared *c*.1900, two separate buildings covered in virginia creeper. In 1930 the property changed hands from the Hopers to Lt.-Col. Arthur Mieville, DSO, MC. It was altered at this time. The porch and oriel window were taken from The Lodge, Littlehampton, which was being demolished to make way for the Odeon Cinema. The porch and window were re-erected at Cudlow House to enable the two buildings to be joined.

**134** The *Marigolds Hotel* in Holmes Lane, *c*.1910. Built in 1889 for C.D. and Miss Mary Hamilton. A fire started by troops during the 1939/45 war destroyed the east wing. The remaining building was demolished on 18 December 1962. Marigolds Lodge was built in its stead in 1963. The ancient Holmes Lane derives its name from Holmes Leaze — 'Holmes', riverside land, higher ground amid marshes (e.g. Mewsbrook), and 'Leaze' — common right of pasturage on the common (e.g. South Field Common). In 1780, the land on both sides of Holmes Lane was called Holmes Leaze Furlong, being within the South Field Common.

**135** Cudlow Parade, *c*.1932, showing Cudlow Cottage and the parade of new shops on the left. Opposite is Hobbs Farm, with the cattle taking centre stage in the road. Also shown is the new Cudlow Avenue, cut between the shops and cottage.

**136** Sea Lane, 1930, shows Morrallee's newspaper shop that had moved from The Street, and The Central Garage, whose proprietor was Mr. Fane Sewell. Behind the flint wall and trees on the left was the property known as The Grange, home of Miss Ethel Urlin.

**137** The *Lamb Inn* corner, 1951, looking south down Sea Lane.

**138** Carriage and pair viewed from the *Lamb Inn,* looking east, up The Street. On the left was Quakers Smith's Church Farm. That in 1905 became C.J. Drake, builder's office and carpenter's shop. The old barn housed traps and carriages kept for hire.

**139** Laying the gas main, 1906. The Littlehampton Gas Company at work in The Street, near Church Farm Cottage, to the evident delight of so many local children.

**140** Church Farm Cottage, *c*.1905. Children at play on pony traps, standing in the coach yard, adjoining the cottage in The Street.

**141** Vincent's grocery store, 1914, on the corner of Church Road and The Street. Mr. Stanford took over the shop in the early 1920s and continued the grocery business there until the 1960s. The aroma of fresh ground coffee pervaded the atmosphere around this little shop.

**142**  The village centre, 1920. The church school is on the left, and Vincent's grocery store on the right. Mr. Vincent's car is parked outside.

**143**  Victoria Farm Dairy, *c*.1948, which was run by the Allison family. It stood on the east side of Church Road, opposite the church in The Street. They sold dairy produce, and you could sit on the forecourt and enjoy their most delicious home-made ice cream, milk-shakes and fruit sundaes. This is now the premises of a solicitor.

**144** Prince of Wales Fund, 1914/15. Boys from the village school, watched by four girls in The Red Cross, are about to march around the village, starting from Church Road. They were collecting for 'The Prince of Wales Fund', proceeds of which were used for giving comforts to servicemen.

**145** Church Farm Cottage, a view looking east down The Street, *c*.1920. The Street remained virtually unchanged, until the new shopping parades were built in the 1950s.

**146** Broadway Mansions, on the corner of Claigmar Road and The Street, was built by Tom Summers in 1909. Many well-known businesses were associated with these shops; Ockenden's hardware, Tuenon's chemists, Gladys Brown's wool shop, Yeates greengrocers, Dormand's butchers, Wingfield The Fisheries and R. & I. Stacey's to name a few. The mansions and flats above were demolished in 1973, and replaced with a building uncharacteristic of Rustington which now houses the controversial Post Office.

**147** The Street, *c*.1956, totally unrecognisable today. The No.66 Southdown bus turns round by the war memorial in Claigmar Road. Centre right, elm trees surround Clock House Fields, where church fêtes and garden parties were once held. On the left, trees hide Dunnabie/Glenthorne, The Chawtons and The Croft, three residences lost for the development of the new shops, which now line both sides of The Street.

**148** The Quix Garage stood for a short period just to the east of Broadway Mansions. The Boxing Day pram race used to end here with the presentation of prizes. It was also used by the local archery club, *c*.1960.

**149** Dunnabie, built in 1909 as Church House by Mr. Jarrett. Subsequently let and later purchased by the Misses Spalding, who turned it into a guest house. During the 1939/45 war it was requisitioned by troops. After hostilities ceased, the house was purchased by Miss Kathleen Bowler and used as a private school. The house was renamed Glenthorne, and in 1963 it was demolished.

**150** The Chawtons was built for the Humphrey family, and Mrs. Sarah Jane Humphrey, the village school mistress, lived here. The house was named after the home of author Jane Austen, who lived in Steventon, Hampshire, and was demolished in 1963.

**151** The Croft, a lovely double-fronted house, built in The Street during 1896 for Mr. F.C. Chappell, a piano manufacturer. In 1911, Dr. Crosbie Walch, the first resident doctor, came to live here. He was followed by Dr. Ernest Walthen Waller. Surely none of his patients will ever forget him, nor his Victorian waiting-room. This house was also demolished when the Churchill Parade was built.

**152** The Street, *c.*1893, looking west, the 'olde worlde' part of the village. Left foreground is Jessamine Cottage, with its adjacent barn and yards. The Vinery and also The Firs, once known as Old Orchard and now Croesswdy, are in the background.

**153** Children in The Street. The Mitchell and Lidbetter children, from nearby cottages, pose for photographs. Nearby is the footpath that led across the fields to Worthing Road, which was later opened up as Old Manor Road. Behind the children is Elm Farm House, *c.*1900.

**154** The village pound was built to house stray animals but seldom used. It adjoins Pound Cottage in The Street. The pound can be seen on Goodwood Estate maps of *c*.1780, before the cottage was built. It appears to have been rebuilt by the Lord of the Manor, Mr. W. Gratwicke, in 1800.

**155**  Artists and photographers all stop here to record these picturesque cottages. In 1780 Garden Cottage is recorded as a wood house for 'Mitchell's Cottage'. This photograph was taken before they were enlarged in 1920.

**156** The Street, looking east. On the right can be seen one of the deep ditches which once networked the village. The banks of these ditches were mossy, and in the springtime were covered with primroses. How peaceful The Street appears, *c*.1930s.

**157** A farming community, *c*.1900. The farmer at work with two well turned out cart-horses. They pause for a picture in The Street, outside ffynches Lodge and West Court Field, now the West Court Health Centre.

**158** Wendy Ridge. When the first houses were built in 1930, the road was called Windy Ridge. Estate agents for obvious reasons advised the current name.

**159** North Lane, the south end in 1932. On the left is the entrance to Mr. Beal's house, called Brendon. It was demolished to allow for the development of Brendon Way. In the background can be seen one of the houses in Wendy Ridge.

**160** ABC Corner, *c.*1925. Norway Cottages, divided into three (A, B, C), were built for the staff of Rustington House. The corner gets its name from the cottages which were later known as Moot House. During the 1939/45 war, this was the H.Q. for canteens run by the W.V.S. and supplied 15 other canteens with all their requirements, except food.

**161** Rustington House was built *c.*1822 for one of the major land-owners in the village, squire Edward Greenfield Penfold. It remained in his family until 1908. Owners up to the 1939/45 war were Miss Hamilton, Sir Malcolm Fox, and Sir George and Lady Hutchinson. It was requisitioned by the military during the war. Since then Mr. Easter, The Electrical Trades Union (as a convalescent home), Rustington House School and Summerlea School, until its closure in 1986, owned the property. It is now occupied by The Hargreaves Construction Company.

**162** Kenny's Cash Stores, *c.*1926. Mr. and Mrs. Kenny stand outside their shop on the corner of Wallace Road and Worthing Road. It was also at one time a sub-post office.

**163** Wallace Road viewed from Worthing Road in 1920. It shows The Beaulau Bakery on the right-hand side of the road.

**164**  Rustington Silver Band muster ready for the armistice procession 1918.

**165**  Armistice procession in Shaftesbury Road. The procession was led by Miss Dorothy Yeates on her white horse. The Yeates family kept a greengrocer's shop in Broadway Mansions, from 1909 when they were first built until *c*.1963.

**166** Carnival float, *c*.1903. Rustington was always renowned for its carnivals, and every one in the village participated in some way. When one carnival was over, the next one was being planned. Here we see a float outside *The Lamb Inn*, where the procession usually formed. The marshal was Mr. Charles J. Drake.

**167** Lady of the lamp. Red Cross float depicting 'Her first patient', which is a spaniel dog having its leg bandaged. Florence Nightingale died on 13 August 1910, aged 90 and the photograph dates from that year.

**168** Carnival in Ash Lane passing Palm Cottage, the home of Thomas Chatfield, the wheelwright. On the right can be seen a sale board, advertising the sale of land at Church Farm in 1903.

**169** Carnival excitement outside *The Lamb Inn*, where the crowds gather in expectation. Note the American flag at the rear, probably due to the late American aerodrome in Rustington. The money raised was in aid of The Littlehampton Cottage Hospital and The Worthing Infirmary.

**170** *(top right)* Rustington football team in the 1928/29 season, when they were cup winners. Back row (left to right), hon. sec. Mr. Atterbury, Alf Balchin, Les Sopp, A. Bushby, Frank Hoare, Mr. Stoner; Middle row, George Tickner, Sid Atterbury, Cecil Fairs, Eddie Woolven; Front row, Mr. Lane, N. Megenis, George Stanbridge and 'Shirty' Lee.

**171** *(right)* Rustington cricket team, *c.*1906. Back row (left to right), Mr. Parmenas Farmener (umpire), Robert Waller, H. Neal, Frank Hoare, Mr. A.H. Shotter, Alan Hoare, Jack MacDonald, Dan Shepherd, Mr. Read; Centre row, James Hoare, Horace Booker, Ernie Sewell, Jack Parsons; Front, seated, George Field.

**172** Silver Jubilee Day, 6 May 1935. The celebrations for King George V and Queen Mary started with a small service, held in the old sports pavilion at the recreation ground. The service was taken by the Rev. J. Louis Crosland, vicar of Rustington parish church.

**173** Coronation Day, 12 May 1937. Police Constable Chappell stands alongside Dr. Waller, who was judging the fancy dress parade, part of the day's celebrations.

**174** Carpenters Convalescent Home. The committee, at a meeting on 8 February 1937, arranged for the home to be floodlit as part of the celebrations for the coronation of King George VI. The matron was authorised to spend up to £5 on prizes for a whist drive, as well as providing a special dinner.

**175** Opening of the village hall. The hall was officially opened on 12 October 1938 by Mr. C.D. Pinchin; he and his wife had given generously to the village hall fund. The hall was dedicated to the memory of those who fell during the 1914/18 war and also commemorated the silver jubilee of King George V and Queen Mary.

**176** Coronation carnival princess, 1953. Miss Sheila Van Damm, the racing driver, presents the winning contestant, Miss Joyce White, with her sash. Her attendants were, from left to right, Miss Trudi Taunton and Miss Patricia Fripp.

**177** *(top right)* Elizabethan dancers, led by the coronation carnival princess and her attendants, in the recreation ground, 2 June 1953.

**178** *(right)* Members of the Littlehampton bonfire society are introduced to the carnival princess, 2 June 1953. They all took part in a procession around the village.

**179** *(left)*   The square dance float, part of the coronation carnival procession, passing down Sea Lane. George Kilhams is at the wheel of the tractor.

**180** *(below left)*   The infant welfare float depicted 'The old woman who lived in a shoe'.

**181** *(below)*   Fancy dress contestants taking part in one of the festivities held on coronation day. Other events were baby shows, Elizabethan, maypole and square dancing displays, sports, a donkey derby, and many side-shows. After a procession around the village, there was dancing for the public, organised by The Rustington Country Dancing Club. Following the Queen's broadcast speech, there was more dancing, this time to the Rustington Square Dance Club. A torch-light procession, starting at 10.30 p.m., ended proceedings for the day.

**182**   The torch-light procession passing *The Lamb Inn*. The car was driven by Mr. Len Nolan, one of the coronation carnival committee, and carried the princess and her attendants, leading the procession, which was watched by many hundreds of people.

# Index

Roman numerals refer to pages in the introduction, and arabic numerals to individual illustrations.

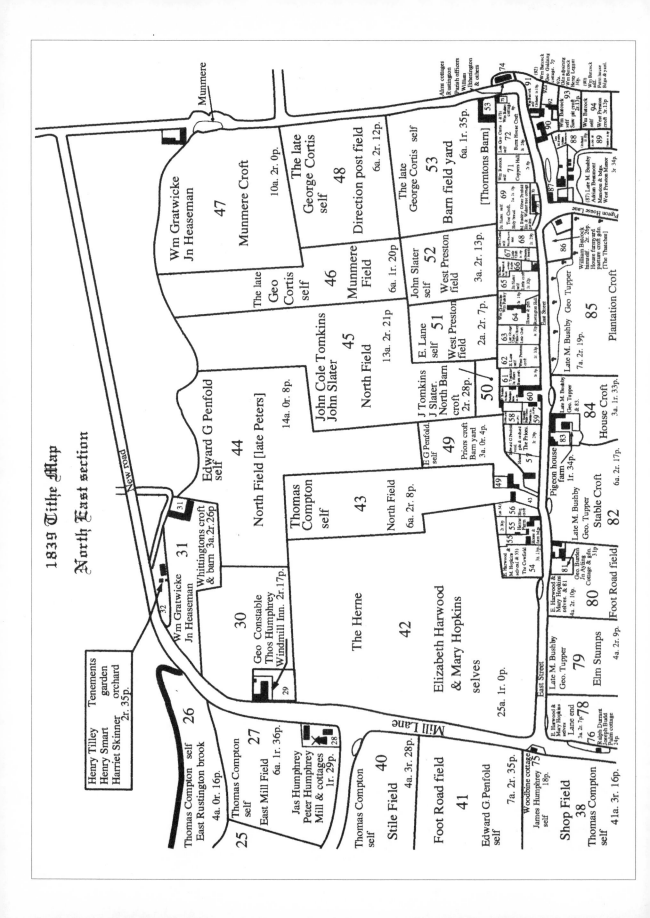

1839 Tithe Map

North East section

Munmere

Henry Tilley Henry Smart Harriet Skinner
Tenements garden orchard 2r. 35p.

Thomas Compton self East Rustington brook
4a. 0r. 16p.
26

Thomas Compton self
East Mill Field
6a. 1r. 36p.
27
25

Jas Humphrey Peter Humphrey Mill & cottages 1r. 29p.
29

Thomas Compton self
Stile Field
4a. 3r. 28p.
40

James Humphrey self
Woodbine cottage 75 18p.
7a. 2r. 35p.

Foot Road field
41

Edward G Penfold self
41a. 3r. 16p.

Thomas Compton self
Shop Field
38

E. Harwood & Mary Hopkins selves
Lane end 78
3a. 2r. 7p. 76
Ralph Durrant Joseph Budd Palm cottage 24p.

Late M. Bushby Geo. Tupper
79
Elm Stumps
80
Foot Road field
4a. 2r. 9p.

Late M. Bushby Geo. Tupper
Stable Croft
82
6a. 2r. 17p.

Geo. Burden Jn Ayling Cottage & gdn. 31p.
81

E. Harwood & Mary Hopkins selves & 81
4a. 2r. 10p.

Elizabeth Harwood & Mary Hopkins selves
25a. 1r. 0p.

The Herne
42

Geo Constable Thos Humphrey Windmill Inn. 2r. 17p.
30

Wm Gratwicke Jn Heaseman
31
Whittingtons croft & barn 3a. 2r. 26p.
32
31

New road

Edward G Penfold self
North Field [late Peters]
44
14a. 0r. 8p.

Thomas Compton self
North Field
43
6a. 2r. 8p.

R. Harwood & M. Hopkins selves( & 55)
The Cowfield
54 3a. 1r. 13p.

55
55
56
56

49
43

E G Penfold self
49
Prions croft Barn yard
3a. 0r. 4p.

Edw G Penfold void gdn. & orchard & 57 The Priors
58
57 1r. 29p.

59
60
50
2r. 28p.
J Tomkins J Slater. North Barn croft

61
62
63
64
65

John Cole Tomkins John Slater
North Field
45
13a. 2r. 21p.

The late Geo Cortis self
46
6a. 1r. 20p.

Munmere Field

E. Lane self
51
West Preston field
2a. 2r. 7p.

John Slater self
52
West Preston field
3a. 2r. 13p.

66
67
68
69
70

71
72

Wm Gratwicke Jn Heaseman
47

Munmere Croft
10a. 2r. 0p.

The late George Cortis self
48

Direction post field
6a. 2r. 12p.

The late George Cortis self
53

Barn field yard
6a. 1r. 35p.

[Thorntons Barn]

53

Alms cottages Rustington Parish officers William Etherington & others

73
91
74

90
92

87

89
88

93
94

Wm Batcock self
Orchard 1 14p.

Wm Batcock Geo Gladding cottage 3y
Gdn adjoining Wm Batcock Hog & goat 34p.
Wm Batcock self Farm house Bldgs & yard.
Wm Preston croft 3r. 33p.

Wm Batcock self
Saw pit croft 2r.13p.

Coppers Hall

Mt. Bushby Oliver Penfold Ho. & Water Ine cottage

Late M. Bushby Adrian Beaumont Mansion & bldgs. West Preston Manor
3r. 34p.

Pigeon House Lane

Late M. Bushby Geo Tupper
85
Plantation Croft
7a. 2r. 19p.

William Batcock himself Pasture croft gdn. House farmyard 2r. 26p. ('The Thatches')

86

Pigeon house farm 1r. 34p.
83

Late M. Bushby Geo. Tupper & 83.
84
House Croft
3a. 1r. 33p.

East Street